Vultures: Nature's Silent Guardians

MD Sharr

Published by pinky, 2024.

While every precaution has been taken in the preparation of this book, the publisher assumes no responsibility for errors or omissions, or for damages resulting from the use of the information contained herein.

VULTURES: NATURE'S SILENT GUARDIANS

First edition. October 8, 2024.

Copyright © 2024 MD Sharr.

ISBN: 979-8227322876

Written by MD Sharr.

Table of Contents

Preface 1
1. The Guardians of the Sky: Vultures 4
2. Vulture Reproduction and Life Cycle 8
3. Vulture Chick Development 12
4. Vulture Family Dynamics 16
5. The Lifespan of Vultures 20
6. Geographical Distribution and Habitat 24
7. Global Population of Vultures 29
8. Vulture Species: A Global Overview 34
9. The Role of Vultures in the Ecosystem 39
10. Vulture Conservation: Challenges and Efforts 43
11. Vultures in Specific Countries 48
12. Interesting Facts about Vultures 53
13. Vultures in History and Mythology 57
14. Stories and Anecdotes about Vultures 61
15. Conclusion: The Future of Vultures 65

Preface

Vultures, often misunderstood and frequently overlooked, are among the most fascinating and important creatures in the natural world. For many, these scavenging birds conjure up images of death and decay, circling ominously in the sky, waiting to feast on the remains of fallen animals. Yet, behind this grim reputation lies a far more complex and vital story—a story of survival, balance, and the intricate relationship between life and death in the ecosystems we all depend on.

This book, "Vultures: Nature's Silent Guardians," has been written to shine a much-needed light on these incredible birds, exploring their vital role in the world and the deep connection they have with human cultures, both past and present. It seeks to answer important questions: Why are vultures so essential to the health of our planet? What challenges do they face today? And most importantly, what can we do to protect them from the threats that endanger their survival?

In recent decades, vultures have been pushed to the brink of extinction in many regions due to a variety of human activities, including habitat destruction, poisoning, and the use of harmful veterinary drugs. Yet, despite their plight, vultures continue to play a critical role in ecosystems, acting as nature's cleanup crew by preventing the spread of disease and maintaining ecological balance. This book aims to foster a deeper understanding and appreciation of vultures and to inspire action to ensure their future survival.

Why was this book written?

This book was written because vultures, though often feared or misunderstood, are one of the most important yet underappreciated animals on Earth. Their ability to consume decaying carcasses without falling ill makes them essential to preventing the spread of deadly diseases like anthrax, rabies, and botulism. As scavengers, vultures clean up the environment, ensuring that ecosystems remain healthy and disease-free. However, despite their indispensable role, vultures are in grave danger of extinction due to the actions of humans. With populations in decline across many regions, it became clear that more needed to be done to raise awareness about vultures and the critical work they do.

This book aims to dispel common myths and misconceptions about vultures and highlight the urgent need for their conservation. Many people view vultures as dirty, sinister, or ominous birds, but nothing could be further from the truth. In reality, they are among the most efficient and clean creatures in the natural world, playing a vital role in recycling nutrients and maintaining the health of ecosystems. By bringing their true nature into focus, this book hopes to change the way people think about vultures and to inspire readers to become advocates for their protection.

What is in this book?

The book covers a wide range of topics about vultures, from their unique adaptations to their fascinating behavior and the critical role they play in the natural world. The chapters take readers on a journey through the lives of these birds, exploring their reproduction, feeding habits, family dynamics, and geographical distribution. Along the way, readers will discover fascinating facts about vultures, such as their incredible sense of smell, which allows them to detect carrion from miles away, and their ability to survive on rotting flesh that would be deadly to other animals.

The book also delves into the rich history and cultural significance of vultures, examining how these birds have been revered and feared by different civilizations throughout history. From the sacred vultures of ancient Egypt, seen as protectors of the pharaohs, to the sky burials of Tibet, where vultures are viewed as spiritual guides, this book explores the deep and often complex relationship between humans and vultures. It also addresses how vultures have been depicted in art, literature, and religion, offering a fascinating glimpse into how these birds have shaped human culture over time.

Moreover, the book presents powerful stories of human-vulture interactions, ranging from village anecdotes to scientific research, and highlights the efforts being made worldwide to conserve vulture populations. Readers will learn about successful conservation programs, such as the breeding and reintroduction efforts that saved the California condor from the brink of extinction, and the vulture restaurants in Europe and Asia that provide safe food sources for vultures.

Why should readers read this book?

Readers should read this book because it offers a fresh perspective on one of the most important yet misunderstood creatures in the animal kingdom. Vultures play a critical role in keeping our planet clean and healthy, and without them, the natural world—and human life—would suffer tremendously. The loss of vultures in some regions has already led to significant increases in disease, highlighting just how crucial these birds are to maintaining ecological balance.

In a world where biodiversity is under constant threat, it is more important than ever to understand and appreciate the roles that different species play in maintaining the health of ecosystems. This book offers readers the opportunity to do just that, providing a detailed yet accessible exploration of vultures and their place in the natural world. Whether you are a nature enthusiast, a conservationist, or simply curious about these remarkable birds, this book will broaden your understanding and appreciation of vultures and their vital contributions to the environment.

"Vultures: Nature's Silent Guardians" is not just a book about birds; it is a call to action. By learning about the challenges vultures face and the solutions that can help them, readers will be empowered to join the global effort to protect these birds and ensure that they continue to soar in the skies for generations to come.

—**Author**

1. The Guardians of the Sky: Vultures

Vultures are more than just birds that feast on death; they are a vital part of life itself. Their role in the ecosystem, cleaning up what others leave behind, ensures that life can continue without disease or decay. While they may not always be welcomed with open arms, their cultural significance and the lessons they offer about nature's cycles are as vast and complex as the skies they soar through.

Overview of Vultures

Vultures, often viewed with a mix of awe and unease, are one of nature's most efficient scavengers. These large, broad-winged birds are known for their ability to soar high in the sky, scanning the ground below for signs of decay. Unlike most birds of prey, vultures don't hunt for fresh kills but instead thrive on dead and decomposing animals, making them vital in maintaining balance within ecosystems.

There are two primary groups of vultures: the Old World vultures, found across Africa, Europe, and Asia, and the New World vultures, which inhabit North and South America. Despite their similar behaviors, these two groups are not closely related, having evolved independently through a phenomenon known as convergent evolution. This means they developed similar features and roles due to the common demands of their environments, not because of shared ancestry.

Vultures come in various shapes and sizes, from the small Egyptian vulture to the massive Andean condor. They are easily recognized by their bald heads, which serve an important purpose. By having no feathers on their heads, vultures avoid bacteria from rotting carcasses getting trapped on them, which helps prevent infection. These birds have exceptional eyesight, enabling them to spot a meal from miles away, and their strong digestive systems allow them to consume carrion that might be harmful to other animals. In short, they are the cleanup crew of nature, ensuring that nothing goes to waste and diseases do not spread.

Importance in the Ecosystem

Vultures are unsung heroes in the natural world. Their primary role is as scavengers, consuming the remains of dead animals that would otherwise rot and attract harmful bacteria, parasites, and diseases. By doing so, vultures help prevent the spread of deadly pathogens such as anthrax, rabies, and botulism, which thrive in decaying flesh. Their unique digestive systems can neutralize these dangerous microbes, making vultures a critical component of healthy ecosystems.

Without vultures, carcasses would linger, attracting more pests, which can lead to an increase in disease transmission, not only among animals but potentially to humans as well. In regions where vulture populations have declined, studies have shown an increase in feral dog populations and rats, which feed on the same carrion. These species, however, lack the same disease resistance, leading to higher incidences of diseases spreading through bites or contaminated environments.

Vultures' scavenging also plays a role in controlling predator behavior. For instance, when a large animal dies, it might attract dangerous carnivores like lions or hyenas, which compete for the carcass. Vultures, with their ability to devour the remains quickly and efficiently, limit the availability of food for these predators, thus reducing conflict and maintaining a balance in predator populations.

Despite their importance, vultures face numerous threats, including habitat destruction, poisoning from human activities, and collisions with power lines. In certain regions, farmers use poison to kill livestock predators, but vultures inadvertently consume the poison-laced carcasses, leading to devastating population declines. It's ironic that while vultures clean the land, they are increasingly finding fewer safe spaces to live.

Cultural and Symbolic Significance

Vultures have represented a variety of ideas and concepts in various cultures throughout history, some more positive than negative. Vultures were honoured as representations of maternity and protection in ancient Egypt. The goddess Nekhbet, who is frequently shown as a vulture, was the pharaoh's defender and the watchdog over Upper Egypt. In ancient paintings and murals, the vulture's extended wings were shown as a mother's embrace, offering solace and protection. Given that vultures are known to be fiercely protective of their young, this relationship most likely developed from the bird's nursing tendencies.

Vultures are important in Tibetan culture because they are used in sky burials, a funeral custom in which the deceased's body is given to vultures. This tradition is predicated on the understanding that life is fleeting and that it is crucial to restore the body to nature as closely as possible. Regarded as sacred animals that facilitate soul liberation, vultures represent the relationship between life, death, and the natural world.

However, not all symbolism attached to vultures is positive. In Western folklore and popular culture, vultures are often seen as harbingers of death, doom, or misfortune, possibly because they are usually found circling over dying or dead animals. Their grim reputation has been reinforced by literature and film, where they are often portrayed as ominous figures lurking on the fringes of life. But this portrayal does them a great disservice, overshadowing their vital role in the circle of life. Across Africa, vultures are sometimes seen as birds with magical properties. In certain cultures, it's believed that consuming vulture body parts can give people supernatural abilities, such as the power to see into the future. Unfortunately, these beliefs have contributed to the illegal trade of vultures, further threatening their already vulnerable populations.

Despite these mixed cultural views, vultures remain creatures of deep significance. Whether revered or feared, they reflect humanity's complex relationship with life, death, and the natural world. Their presence is a reminder of nature's delicate balance and the interconnectedness of all species. These majestic scavengers, with their efficient, sometimes misunderstood ways, continue to play an essential role in keeping our world healthy.

2. Vulture Reproduction and Life Cycle

Vultures may not be known for their beauty or grace, but their reproductive cycle is a testament to their resilience and the strength of their family bonds. Through careful courtship, dedicated incubation, and extended care for their chicks, vultures ensure that their species continues to play its vital role in the ecosystem for generations to come.

Mating and Courtship Behavior

Vultures may seem like solitary creatures as they soar through the sky, but when it comes to mating and courtship, they display remarkable coordination and companionship. Most vulture species form monogamous pairs, meaning they choose a partner and remain together throughout their lives. These bonds are essential for ensuring the survival of their offspring.

Courtship among vultures involves intricate displays and behaviors that signal their readiness to mate. A pair of vultures often engage in a "sky dance," where they soar together in a series of aerial maneuvers. This graceful flight may include diving, circling, and sometimes locking talons mid-air. On the ground, vultures show affection by nuzzling and grooming each other. Mating rituals also involve vocalizations that are specific to each species, with some vultures making soft calls or engaging in wing-spreading displays to signal interest.

One of the most interesting aspects of vulture courtship is their site fidelity. They often return to the same nesting locations year after year, sometimes even to the exact same nest. These locations are usually isolated, high-up spots like cliffs or tall trees, where they can safely raise their young. By establishing strong, lifelong bonds, vultures ensure they have a reliable partner for raising their chicks, a task that requires teamwork and dedication.

Pregnancy: How Vultures Reproduce

Vultures, like all birds, reproduce through the process of laying eggs. Once a pair of vultures has completed their courtship rituals, they engage in mating, which usually takes place at or near their nesting site. Unlike mammals, vultures do not experience pregnancy in the traditional sense, as they do not carry their offspring internally. Instead, their reproductive cycle leads to the development of eggs within the female.

Once fertilization occurs, the female's body prepares to lay eggs by producing thick-shelled eggs that can withstand the external environment. Vultures typically lay only one or two eggs per breeding season, a trait that makes their reproductive strategy more focused on quality over quantity. The large size of their eggs ensures that their young are well-developed when they hatch.

Reproduction in vultures is highly dependent on environmental conditions. The availability of food and the safety of their nesting site both play critical roles in determining the success of their breeding. For many species of vultures, the breeding season coincides with periods when food is more abundant, ensuring that both parents have the energy to care for their chick once it hatches.

Egg Laying: Timing and Frequency

Vultures do not lay eggs frequently. In most species, the female vulture will lay one egg per breeding season, though some may occasionally lay two. Egg-laying usually occurs in the early part of the breeding season, which can vary depending on the region and species. In temperate climates, vultures often breed in late winter or early spring, while tropical species may breed during the rainy season when food is more plentiful.

The timing of egg-laying is carefully synchronized with the availability of resources, as the parents will need to provide food and protection to their chick. Once the egg is laid, the female settles into her nest, which is often a large, untidy structure built from sticks, bones, and vegetation. Vultures prefer remote, inaccessible locations for their nests, such as cliffs or tall trees, to keep their eggs safe from predators.

The eggs are typically large and pale in color, sometimes with brown or gray spots. The female and male take turns incubating the egg, ensuring it is kept warm and protected at all times. Both parents are actively involved in the care of their offspring, a key factor in ensuring the chick's survival.

Incubation Period: Days Until Eggs Hatch

The incubation period for vulture eggs varies slightly by species, but it typically lasts between 45 to 60 days. During this time, the parent vultures take turns sitting on the egg, keeping it warm and turning it regularly to ensure even development. Incubation is a time of patience and diligence, as both parents must remain close to the nest to protect the egg from harsh weather conditions or potential predators.

Vultures show an incredible level of commitment during this period. Even though they share the incubation duties, the pair is never far from their nest. Their dedication helps ensure that the egg remains in optimal conditions for hatching. During these weeks, the adult vultures must also find time to feed themselves, but they take turns, with one bird staying at the nest while the other searches for food.

As the incubation period draws to a close, the parents become even more attentive, waiting for signs that their chick is ready to emerge. The chick inside the egg begins to prepare for the hatching process, using a small, specialized structure called an "egg tooth" to peck its way out of the eggshell.

The Hatching Process and Early Life of Vulture Chicks

When the time comes for the chick to hatch, the process is slow and requires a great deal of effort. The chick uses its egg tooth to break through the shell in a process known as "pipping." This can take several hours or even days, as the chick must rest between attempts to chip away at the shell. During this time, the parent vultures remain close, ready to assist if necessary.

Once the chick finally breaks free from the egg, it is weak, covered in downy feathers, and completely dependent on its parents. The first few days of a vulture chick's life are critical. The parents take turns feeding the chick, regurgitating food that they've collected during their scavenging flights. The chick remains in the nest for several months, during which time it rapidly grows and develops the strength needed to fly.

Vulture chicks grow relatively slowly compared to other bird species, and they require extended care from their parents. They remain in the nest for up to six months, during which time both parents continue to provide food and protection. The young vultures practice flapping their wings and building their strength, but they are not ready to leave the nest until they are fully fledged.

As they prepare to take their first flight, young vultures must learn the skills that will enable them to survive on their own. They start by practicing short flights from the nest, gradually increasing their distance as they gain confidence. By the time they leave the nest, they are fully equipped to begin their life as scavengers, soaring high in the sky just like their parents.

3. Vulture Chick Development

The journey from a helpless chick to a soaring adult is one of dedication and gradual learning for vultures. Their early life is marked by close parental care, careful feeding, and the development of critical survival skills. Each stage of their growth brings them closer to becoming the skilled scavengers that help maintain the balance in nature. While their journey to independence takes time, vultures are a testament to the patience and resilience that is essential for thriving in the wild.

Diet of Vulture Chicks: What They Eat

From the moment a vulture chick hatches, its survival depends on the careful care and feeding provided by its parents. Unlike many bird species that feed their chick seeds or insects, vulture chicks are raised on a diet of regurgitated carrion, just like the adults. This diet of decaying animal flesh might sound unappealing, but for vultures, it's essential for growth and development.

The parents take turns scavenging for food, often flying long distances to find the remains of dead animals. Once they have filled their stomachs with carrion, they return to the nest and regurgitate the food for their chick. The young vulture eagerly accepts this pre-digested meal, which is easier to digest and full of the nutrients it needs to grow. This cycle continues multiple times a day in the early weeks of life, as vulture chicks need frequent feeding to build strength.

As the chick grows, the portions become larger, and the frequency of feeding decreases. Over time, the chick's digestive system adapts to handle the tougher, less processed parts of the carrion. The parents gradually introduce more solid pieces of meat, helping the chick adjust to the type of food it will eventually eat as an adult.

Growth Stages: From Hatchling to Juvenile

A vulture chick's life begins in the safety of its nest, typically located on a high, rocky cliff or in the branches of a tall tree. When they first hatch, vulture chicks are covered in soft, downy feathers and are entirely dependent on their parents for warmth, protection, and food. At this stage, they are helpless, and unable to move much or regulate their body temperature, so the parents must remain nearby to keep them warm.

In the early days, the chick spends most of its time sleeping and eating, allowing its body to grow rapidly. Within a few weeks, the fluffy down feathers begin to be replaced by stronger, darker feathers, which are better suited for life outside the nest. This stage marks the beginning of the chick's transition from a hatchling to a juvenile. The chick becomes more active, moving around the nest and stretching its growing wings.

By the time the chick reaches two to three months of age, it starts resembling an adult vulture, though it is still smaller and less coordinated. Its body is now covered in proper feathers, and it becomes more curious about its surroundings. This juvenile phase is a time of exploration and practice, where the young vulture begins to mimic its parents' behaviors, such as flapping its wings and observing their flight patterns.

Learning to Fly: Age When Vultures Begin Flight

One of the most critical milestones in a vulture chick's life is learning to fly. This process is known as fledging, and it usually occurs when the chick is around three to six months old, depending on the species. For weeks before their first flight, young vultures practice flapping their wings vigorously while remaining in the safety of the nest. This wing exercise helps strengthen their muscles and prepares them for the moment they take their first leap into the air.

At first, fledging can be a nerve-wracking experience for the young vulture. Some may make short, clumsy hops from the nest to nearby branches or rocks, gradually building their confidence and coordination. The parents continue to watch over the chick during this time, sometimes encouraging it to fly by calling to it from a distance or demonstrating their own soaring abilities.

Once the young vulture takes its first proper flight, it is still far from being an expert flyer. It may take several more weeks of practice to master the art of soaring, gliding, and using thermals (rising warm air currents) to stay aloft with minimal effort. Vultures are known for their ability to travel great distances in search of food, and this skill of efficient flight is essential for survival. During this learning period, the chick may continue to return to the nest for food, as it is not yet capable of fully fending for itself.

Independence: Transition from Chick to Adult

The transition from chick to adult is a gradual process for vultures. Even after they learn to fly, young vultures often remain near their parents for several more months. This extended period of dependency allows the juvenile vulture to learn essential survival skills, such as finding food, avoiding predators, and navigating their environment.

During this time, the young vulture continues to grow stronger, gaining weight and developing the sharp eyesight and keen senses that vultures are known for. It begins to join its parents on scavenging trips, where it learns how to spot potential food sources from high in the sky. The juvenile also observes how adult vultures interact with other members of their species, learning social behaviors that will help them integrate into larger groups of vultures later in life.

By the time the young vulture reaches around six to nine months of age, it is ready to leave the nest and become fully independent. At this point, it has mastered the skills needed to survive on its own. The juvenile no longer relies on its parents for food and can travel long distances to find carrion, just like an adult.

However, even though the young vulture is now capable of independent life, it may not be ready to breed for several more years. Most vulture species reach sexual maturity between four and six years of age. Until then, they continue to hone their scavenging skills, establish their territory, and sometimes join other young vultures in loose social groups. Vultures have a relatively long lifespan, with some species living up to 30 years or more in the wild. This extended lifespan allows them to play a consistent and essential role in their ecosystems. By the time a young vulture reaches adulthood, it is well-prepared to take on the responsibilities of cleaning up the environment and contributing to the survival of its species.

4. Vulture Family Dynamics

Vulture family dynamics are a blend of loyalty, cooperation, and social organization. Whether they mate for life or seasonally, vulture pairs work together in raising their young, sharing the responsibilities of feeding, guarding, and teaching survival skills. Their social structure, particularly around feeding, highlights a mix of competition and cooperation, ensuring that every member of the vulture community has a chance to thrive. In this way, vultures exemplify the importance of balance—within families, communities, and the ecosystems they inhabit.

Family Formation: Mating for Life or Seasonal Partners?
Vultures are known for their loyalty when it comes to choosing a mate. Most species of vultures form strong, long-term pair bonds, and many of them mate for life. Once a vulture finds a partner, the two stay together, often returning to the same nesting sites year after year. This kind of lifelong partnership allows vultures to raise their young with stability, ensuring that both parents work together to provide care and protection for their chicks.

For vultures, mating for life is not just about companionship; it is a practical strategy for survival. By maintaining the same partner over multiple breeding seasons, vultures become highly synchronized in their roles as parents. They know each other's habits, strengths, and weaknesses, which helps them cooperate more effectively when raising their young. This long-term bond also reduces the time spent on courtship, allowing them to focus on finding a safe nesting site and preparing for the arrival of their chicks.

In contrast, some vulture species do not always form lifelong bonds. Certain species may have seasonal partners, where they pair up only during the breeding season and find a new mate in subsequent years. These species still exhibit strong family ties during the nesting period, with both parents working together to raise their offspring, but the partnership may dissolve once the chicks are independent.

Regardless of whether a vulture mates for life or chooses a new partner each season, their commitment to family remains steadfast. The success of their offspring depends heavily on the cooperation and dedication of both parents.

Parental Roles: Division of Labor in Raising Chicks

Vultures are known for their teamwork when it comes to raising their chicks. Both parents share the responsibility of incubation, feeding, and protecting their young. The division of labor within a vulture family is well-balanced, with each parent taking on specific roles to ensure the survival of their chick.

During the incubation period, both the male and female vultures take turns sitting on the egg, keeping it warm and protected from the elements. This shared duty allows the parents to alternate between guarding the nest and searching for food. While one parent incubates the egg, the other flies off in search of carrion, returning with food for themselves and, later, for the chick.

Once the chick hatches, the division of labor becomes even more apparent. Both parents continue to take turns feeding the chick, regurgitating food that they have scavenged from carcasses. This shared feeding responsibility ensures that the chick receives regular nourishment and that neither parent becomes overburdened. The chick's diet is rich in nutrients, thanks to the efforts of both parents to find high-quality food sources.

In addition to feeding, one parent always remains near the nest to guard the chick from predators or other threats. Vulture nests are often located in remote, hard-to-reach places, such as cliffs or tall trees, but predators like eagles, snakes, or other scavengers can still pose a danger. By dividing their duties, vulture parents create a secure environment where the chick can grow without constant risk.

As the chick grows older and becomes more independent, the parents slowly reduce their involvement in feeding, encouraging the young vulture to begin practicing flight and foraging on its own. This gradual transition helps prepare the chick for life as a fully independent scavenger.

Social Structure within Vulture Communities

Vultures are often seen as solitary creatures, gliding through the sky alone or perched on cliffs in remote locations. However, they also exhibit fascinating social behaviors, especially when it comes to feeding and community interactions. Vultures live in loose social groups that are formed around feeding opportunities rather than strict family units, but these groups follow certain social rules that help maintain order and cooperation.

One of the most notable social behaviors among vultures is their feeding hierarchy. When a large carcass is discovered, vultures gather in numbers, often with multiple species converging at the same site. The social structure within these feeding gatherings is determined by size, species, and dominance. Larger vultures, such as the Andean condor or the lappet-faced vulture, tend to eat first, while smaller species, like the Egyptian vulture, wait their turn. This feeding hierarchy ensures that the strongest vultures get their fill first, while smaller or less dominant individuals scavenge for leftovers once the larger birds have finished.

Although feeding times can be competitive, vultures often cooperate with one another when it comes to locating food. Many species use their keen eyesight to watch other vultures, and when one bird spots a carcass, others quickly follow. This cooperative behavior benefits the entire group, as it increases the chances of finding food in harsh environments where meals can be scarce.

Within a vulture community, there is also a level of mutual respect when it comes to nesting sites. Vultures tend to build their nests in areas far away from other species, but in places where multiple pairs may nest close together, they avoid conflict by respecting each other's territories. Even though vultures may not live in tight-knit colonies like some other bird species, there is a shared understanding that allows them to coexist peacefully.

In some cases, vulture communities can extend beyond just family units and feeding groups. Vultures have been observed assisting one another in non-breeding activities, such as scouting for safe roosting spots or helping to defend against predators. While these interactions may not be as frequent as in other social animals, they demonstrate that vultures have a complex social structure that goes beyond simple survival instincts.

Vultures also play a critical role in the larger ecosystem by acting as nature's cleanup crew. Their scavenging habits prevent the spread of disease and help maintain the balance between life and death in the natural world. By working together, whether in raising chicks or feeding on carcasses, vultures contribute to the overall health of their environment.

5. The Lifespan of Vultures

Vultures, with their impressive longevity, are true survivors of the skies. They may face numerous challenges throughout their lives, from food shortages to human interference, but their resilience and adaptability help them thrive in the wild. Whether living for 20, 30, or even 50 years, vultures play an essential role in maintaining the balance of nature, and through conservation efforts, we can ensure that these majestic birds continue to soar for generations to come.

Average Lifespan of Different Vulture Species

Vultures are among the longest-living birds in the animal kingdom, often outliving many of their avian counterparts. However, their lifespan varies across species and environments. On average, most vulture species live between 20 to 30 years in the wild, though some individuals have been known to survive much longer under ideal conditions.

The Andean condor, one of the largest vulture species, has one of the longest lifespans, often living up to 50 years in the wild. In captivity, where threats from predators, food scarcity, and environmental hazards are minimized, these birds can live even longer, with reports of condors reaching up to 70 years in some cases.

Other species, like the griffon vulture and the lappet-faced vulture, typically live for around 30 years in the wild. These birds are well-adapted to their environments and have developed strong survival skills, which contribute to their relatively long lives. Vultures such as the white-backed vulture or the Egyptian vulture also enjoy similar longevity, with lifespans of 20 to 30 years, though, like other species, some individuals in captivity may live significantly longer.

The length of a vulture's life is directly tied to the conditions in which it lives. Birds in protected environments, such as national parks or sanctuaries, often have longer lifespans than those in more hazardous, human-impacted regions. Vultures in the wild face a host of challenges that can shorten their lives, ranging from habitat destruction to food scarcity, but those who survive the early years of life generally have a good chance of reaching an advanced age.

Factors Affecting Vulture Longevity

Several factors influence how long a vulture can live. While genetics play a role in determining a bird's maximum lifespan, external factors, such as food availability, environmental hazards, human interference, and disease, can have a significant impact on a vulture's longevity.

One of the most critical factors affecting vulture lifespan is food availability. Vultures rely on carcasses for sustenance, and in areas where prey animals are abundant, vultures can find plenty to eat. However, in regions where human activity has reduced wildlife populations, vultures may struggle to find enough food. The availability of large animal carcasses, such as those of livestock or wild herbivores, is essential for these scavengers, especially since vultures cannot easily adapt to eating smaller prey. When food is scarce, vultures may face starvation, particularly during harsh seasons or extended droughts.

Human activity has also posed a significant threat to vulture populations, which in turn affects their lifespan. Habitat destruction, whether due to deforestation, agricultural expansion, or urbanization, has encroached on vulture nesting and feeding grounds. As vultures lose access to traditional roosting and breeding sites, they are forced to travel greater distances in search of food and shelter, putting them at greater risk of exhaustion, injury, or death.

Another major factor affecting vulture longevity is poisoning. In many regions, vultures fall victim to secondary poisoning from chemicals intended for other animals. Farmers and herders may use poison to protect livestock from predators like lions or hyenas, but when vultures feed on the carcasses of poisoned animals, they too are affected. One of the most notorious poisons impacting vultures is diclofenac, a veterinary drug used to treat livestock. Vultures that consume the carcasses of animals treated with this drug often suffer fatal kidney failure, leading to drastic declines in vulture populations in certain areas.

In addition to poisoning, vultures are sometimes targeted by poachers, either deliberately or accidentally. In certain cultures, vultures are believed to have mystical or medicinal properties, leading to illegal hunting and the sale of vulture parts on the black market. These practices not only reduce vulture populations but also prevent individuals from reaching their full lifespan.

Diseases and environmental hazards can also take a toll on vulture longevity. While vultures have evolved strong immune systems to protect against the bacteria in rotting carcasses, they are still vulnerable to avian diseases such as bird flu. In areas where disease outbreaks occur, vultures can quickly succumb if they are exposed to infected animals. Additionally, natural hazards such as extreme weather events, wildfires, or landslides can destroy nests and reduce food availability, impacting vulture survival rates.

Despite these challenges, vultures have developed several adaptations that help them live long lives. Their efficient digestive systems allow them to process decaying food without getting sick, and their keen eyesight enables them to spot food from great distances. These traits, combined with their ability to travel long distances in search of food, help vultures survive in even the harshest environments. Furthermore, their social feeding habits—where large groups of vultures gather to consume a carcass—ensure that they can efficiently share resources and minimize the risk of starvation.

However, the key to a long life for vultures lies in the early stages of development. Vultures that survive the vulnerable chick and juvenile stages have a much higher chance of living for decades. Parental care plays an essential role during these early years, with both parents working together to feed and protect their chicks. Once a vulture reaches adulthood, its size, strength, and intelligence help it navigate the challenges of the wild, giving it the resilience to survive for many years.

Conservation efforts have also played a critical role in extending the lifespan of vultures in recent decades. By establishing vulture conservation programs, building vulture restaurants (designated safe feeding areas), and implementing bans on harmful chemicals like diclofenac, organizations, and governments have worked to protect these important birds from the threats they face. These efforts, combined with public awareness campaigns, have helped to stabilize vulture populations in some regions, ensuring that more vultures can live to their full potential.

6. Geographical Distribution and Habitat

Vultures are truly global citizens, adapted to various environments and climates, from the grasslands of Africa to the mountain ranges of South America. Their wide geographical distribution reflects their resilience, but it also underscores the urgent need for conservation to protect these majestic birds. With ongoing efforts to preserve their habitats and prevent threats like poisoning, vultures can continue to fulfill their vital ecological role, cleaning up the world and maintaining the balance of nature.

Native Regions of Vultures

Vultures are remarkable birds that have adapted to a wide range of geographical locations across the globe. These scavengers are native to every continent except Antarctica and Australia, thriving in diverse environments that suit their unique ecological role. There are two primary groups of vultures: the Old World vultures, native to Europe, Africa, and Asia, and the New World vultures, which are found in North and South America. Despite the geographical separation, both groups have evolved to fill similar ecological niches as nature's cleanup crew.

Old World vultures, such as the Egyptian vulture and the griffon vulture, are widely distributed across Europe, North Africa, and parts of Asia. These species tend to be more diverse in terms of their range and can be found in the dry deserts of North Africa to the mountainous regions of the Himalayas. In contrast, New World vultures, such as the Andean condor and the turkey vulture, are native to the Americas, inhabiting regions from the southern United States down to the southern tip of South America.

Vultures have adapted to these varied environments through their keen senses and their ability to travel long distances in search of food. Their wide-ranging distribution across continents shows their incredible adaptability to different climates and terrains.

Habitats Preferred by Different Vulture Species

Although vultures are widespread, each species has specific habitat preferences that suit their survival strategies. These preferences are shaped by the availability of food, nesting sites, and environmental conditions.

Many vulture species prefer open landscapes like grasslands, savannas, and deserts, where they can easily spot carcasses from great distances. For instance, the white-backed vulture is commonly found in the savannas of sub-Saharan Africa, where large herbivores provide a steady supply of carrion. Similarly, the turkey vulture, native to the Americas, thrives in open forests, grasslands, and even semi-arid regions.

Other vultures, like the bearded vulture, are more specialized and live in mountainous areas. The bearded vulture, native to the mountainous regions of Europe and Asia, has adapted to living at high altitudes, where it feeds primarily on bone marrow. These vultures can be seen soaring over steep cliffs and rocky terrains, using the high vantage points to spot their meals.

In contrast, some species prefer forested or semi-forested regions. The king vulture, found in the tropical forests of Central and South America, is a prime example. It uses its strong beak to tear into carcasses that other vultures might not be able to access, and its habitat provides plenty of cover and nesting opportunities.

While vultures are commonly associated with dry, open landscapes, their habitat preferences are diverse. They can be found in rainforests, deserts, mountains, and even coastal areas. This adaptability to various habitats ensures that vultures can survive in a range of environments as long as their primary food source—carcasses—is available.

Current Global Distribution of Vultures

Vultures are globally distributed, but their numbers vary greatly depending on the region. Africa remains the stronghold for many vulture species, with savannas and open woodlands providing ideal conditions for both Old World vultures and large populations. However, vultures are not limited to Africa alone. Europe is home to several species, such as the griffon vulture and the cinereous vulture, which are found in parts of southern Europe, particularly in Spain, where vulture conservation efforts have been successful.

In Asia, vultures are found in countries like India, Nepal, and Pakistan, although their populations have suffered significant declines in recent decades. South Asia, once a thriving region for vultures, has seen catastrophic drops in vulture numbers due to the use of the veterinary drug diclofenac, which is toxic to vultures that feed on treated livestock. Conservation efforts in these areas are now focused on banning the drug and establishing breeding programs to recover vulture populations.

In the Americas, the New World vultures range from southern Canada to the southern tip of South America. The turkey vulture, one of the most widespread vulture species, can be found throughout the Americas, from the forests of the Amazon to the deserts of Mexico and the United States. The Andean condor, another New World vulture, is found primarily in the Andes Mountains of South America, where it plays an essential role in maintaining the ecological balance of these high-altitude ecosystems.

While vultures remain globally distributed, their populations are under increasing pressure from habitat loss, poisoning, and other human activities. Many species are now classified as endangered or critically endangered, with concerted global conservation efforts needed to prevent further declines.

Countries with the Highest Vulture Populations

Several countries stand out for having significant populations of vultures, largely due to favorable habitats and ongoing conservation efforts. Africa remains the continent with the highest vulture populations, particularly in countries like Kenya, Tanzania, and South Africa. These countries offer large expanses of national parks and reserves, where vultures can find food and nesting sites relatively undisturbed by human activity. The Serengeti ecosystem, for example, is home to vast numbers of vultures, including the Rüppell's griffon vulture and the lappet-faced vulture.

In Europe, Spain is known for its robust vulture populations, especially griffon vultures. Conservation measures, including vulture restaurants (designated feeding stations) and protected breeding sites, have helped stabilize and grow vulture populations in the region. Spain's rugged landscapes and mountainous regions provide perfect habitats for these birds.

India, despite suffering severe declines in vulture numbers due to diclofenac poisoning, is still home to some of the world's largest vulture populations. The government's ban on diclofenac and the establishment of vulture breeding centers have led to slow but hopeful recovery efforts. Nepal and Pakistan have also implemented similar bans and are working to restore their vulture populations.

In South America, countries like Argentina, Chile, and Peru are home to large populations of the Andean condor. These nations have prioritized vulture conservation through reintroduction programs and public awareness campaigns. The Andes Mountains serve as a critical habitat for condors, where they play a key role in the ecosystem as scavengers.

In the United States, the turkey vulture is abundant and widespread, found in almost every state. Its adaptability to various environments, from urban areas to remote wilderness, has allowed it to maintain a stable population. Conservation efforts across North and South America have helped protect these birds, ensuring they continue to thrive.

7. Global Population of Vultures

Vultures, though absent from places like Antarctica and Australia, are found across many parts of the world. From the Andean condors of South America to the griffon vultures of Europe and the struggling populations of South Asia, vultures play an essential ecological role in maintaining balance in their respective environments. Despite challenges like habitat loss, poisoning, and human interference, ongoing global conservation efforts aim to protect these majestic birds, ensuring they continue to soar in the skies for future generations.

Vulture Numbers in North America

In North America, vultures are an important part of the ecosystem, primarily represented by two species: the turkey vulture and the black vulture. These species are quite abundant across the continent, with the turkey vulture being especially widespread. Turkey vultures are easily recognized by their red heads and large, dark wings, often seen soaring over open fields and highways.

Turkey vultures are present throughout the United States, southern Canada, and Mexico, and their numbers are stable due to their adaptability to various environments. Black vultures, which have a more restricted range, are primarily found in the southeastern United States and parts of Mexico. Both species benefit from human activity in some ways, often scavenging along roadsides or near agricultural areas.

Though vultures in North America are relatively secure compared to other regions, they are not without threats. Habitat destruction and occasional poisoning incidents do pose risks, but conservation efforts and their ability to thrive in a variety of environments have helped maintain healthy populations.

Vulture Numbers in South America

In South America, the vulture population is dominated by species such as the Andean condor, king vulture, and turkey vulture. The Andean condor, one of the largest flying birds in the world, is particularly iconic in the mountainous regions of the Andes, where it plays a critical role as a scavenger.

The Andean condor population, while not as numerous as some other vulture species, is the subject of numerous conservation programs. These programs aim to protect the bird from habitat loss and poisoning, which have historically reduced its numbers. In some countries, such as Argentina, Chile, and Peru, the Andean condor is a cultural symbol, which has helped spur efforts to preserve it.

Turkey vultures and black vultures are also widespread across South America, particularly in tropical and subtropical regions. These species are more adaptable and have larger populations, often seen soaring over rainforests and open plains. They are a common sight from Brazil to Colombia, playing a vital role in cleaning up the environment.

Vultures in Europe

Europe is home to several vulture species, including the griffon vulture, cinereous vulture, and bearded vulture. Among these, the griffon vulture is the most common and widely distributed, particularly in countries like Spain, France, and Greece. Spain has one of the largest populations of griffon vultures, thanks to successful conservation measures such as feeding stations (vulture restaurants) and legal protections.

The cinereous vulture, also known as the black vulture, is another important species in Europe, found in parts of southern Europe and Central Asia. This species has a more restricted range but has been the focus of significant conservation efforts, especially in Spain and France, where reintroduction programs have been successful in boosting numbers.

The bearded vulture, known for its unique habit of feeding on bone marrow, is found in the mountainous regions of the Alps, Pyrenees, and Balkans. Thanks to international conservation initiatives, this vulture species has made a comeback in recent decades, with populations increasing in places like Switzerland and Austria.

Vultures in Asia

Asia is home to several vulture species, including the white-rumped vulture, Himalayan griffon vulture, and slender-billed vulture. However, the vulture populations in Asia have suffered catastrophic declines over the past few decades, particularly in South Asia. The use of the veterinary drug diclofenac, which is toxic to vultures, has led to significant population crashes in India, Nepal, and Pakistan.

In India, for instance, vulture numbers plummeted by over 90% in the 1990s due to the widespread use of diclofenac in livestock. Vultures that fed on the carcasses of treated animals suffered fatal kidney damage. This decline was especially devastating for species like the white-rumped vulture, once one of the most common birds of prey in the region.

Despite these challenges, there is hope for vultures in Asia. India, Nepal, and Pakistan have implemented bans on the use of diclofenac, and conservation programs, including breeding centers and safe zones, are working to bring vulture populations back from the brink of extinction. In the Himalayan region, the Himalayan griffon vulture remains relatively stable, often seen soaring over the high-altitude landscapes.

Vultures in Antarctica

Vultures are notably absent from Antarctica. The continent's harsh, icy environment provides no suitable habitat for these scavenging birds, as there is little opportunity for them to find food in the form of animal carcasses. Vultures thrive in environments where large terrestrial animals are present, so the frigid and barren conditions of Antarctica are unsuitable for their survival.

While vultures are not found in Antarctica, other scavengers, such as skuas, have adapted to life in the polar regions, relying on the abundant marine life and the occasional opportunities to scavenge from penguin colonies.

Vultures in Australia

Interestingly, Australia is also devoid of vultures. While the continent has a diverse range of bird species, including many raptors, there are no native vultures. Instead, Australia's scavenging birds are represented by species like the wedge-tailed eagle and various corvids (crows and ravens), which fulfill similar ecological roles by cleaning up carrion and keeping the environment free of waste.

Australia's unique wildlife and isolation from other continents likely contributed to the absence of vultures, as the continent evolved its own set of scavengers and predators adapted to its specific environment.

Vultures in India

India has historically been home to some of the largest vulture populations in the world, but as mentioned earlier, these numbers have drastically declined due to the diclofenac crisis. Species such as the white-rumped vulture, Indian vulture, and slender-billed vulture once thrived across the Indian subcontinent, playing a vital role in cleaning up livestock carcasses and preventing the spread of disease.

The loss of vultures in India has had far-reaching consequences. With fewer vultures to consume carcasses, populations of feral dogs and rats have increased, leading to a rise in diseases such as rabies. Recognizing the importance of vultures to public health and the environment, India has become a leader in vulture conservation efforts. Breeding centers, vulture restaurants, and public awareness campaigns are part of the broader effort to restore these essential birds.

8. Vulture Species: A Global Overview

Vultures are truly global birds, found across continents and in a wide range of habitats, from the mountains of South America to the savannas of Africa. Despite their critical ecological role, many species are under threat, and urgent conservation efforts are needed to protect these birds from extinction. As the world becomes more aware of their importance, vultures may yet have a chance to continue soaring in the skies for generations to come.

Number of Vulture Species Worldwide

Vultures are fascinating birds that have evolved to occupy a critical niche in ecosystems around the world. Globally, there are 23 recognized species of vultures, divided into two distinct groups: Old World vultures and New World vultures. Despite their similar scavenging habits, these two groups are not closely related genetically. Instead, they developed similar characteristics through a process called convergent evolution, driven by their shared ecological roles.

Old World vultures belong to the Accipitridae family and are found across Africa, Europe, and Asia. These vultures are more closely related to eagles and hawks. In contrast, New World vultures belong to the Cathartidae family and are found in North and South America. Interestingly, New World vultures are more closely related to storks than to their Old World counterparts, though they share many physical and behavioral traits.

Despite the differences in evolutionary background, vultures around the world serve the same crucial purpose: they consume dead animals and help prevent the spread of disease. Their ability to digest rotting flesh, which contains harmful bacteria, ensures that ecosystems remain clean and free from decaying carcasses. However, despite their importance, vultures face numerous challenges, and many species are now endangered or critically endangered.

Breakdown of Vulture Species by Continent

Africa

Africa is home to some of the most iconic vulture species, many of which are facing severe population declines due to poisoning, habitat loss, and human conflict. There are 11 species of vultures found on the African continent, with some of the most well-known including the white-backed vulture, the lappet-faced vulture, and the hooded vulture.

The white-backed vulture is the most widespread species in sub-Saharan Africa. These vultures prefer savannas and open woodlands, where they can easily spot carrion from above. Unfortunately, the species has seen dramatic declines in recent decades due to poisoning and the illegal wildlife trade.

The lappet-faced vulture, one of Africa's largest vultures, is another iconic species found across the continent. These vultures are often seen at large carcasses, where they use their strong beaks to tear through tough hide that other scavengers cannot manage. Despite their size and strength, lappet-faced vultures are also facing population declines, largely due to habitat destruction and human encroachment.

Europe

In Europe, there are four species of vultures, with the griffon vulture being the most widespread. Found in countries like Spain, France, and Greece, griffon vultures have benefited from conservation efforts that include protected breeding areas and vulture restaurants, where carrion is provided for feeding.

The cinereous vulture, or black vulture, is another significant species in Europe. This vulture can be found in parts of Spain and Central Asia, and it is one of the largest flying birds in the world. Like other vultures in Europe, the cinereous vulture has seen its population increase thanks to focused conservation efforts.

The bearded vulture, also known as the lammergeier, is a unique species found in mountainous regions like the Pyrenees and the Alps. It is famous for its unusual diet of bone marrow, which it extracts by dropping bones from great heights to crack them open.

Asia

Asia is home to several vulture species, though the populations of many of these birds have suffered catastrophic declines, particularly in South Asia. Species such as the white-rumped vulture, slender-billed vulture, and Indian vulture were once among the most common birds of prey in the region. However, their numbers have plummeted due to the widespread use of the veterinary drug diclofenac, which is toxic to vultures that consume the carcasses of treated livestock.

In the Himalayas, the Himalayan griffon vulture remains relatively stable. This large species is often seen soaring over high-altitude landscapes, where it plays a critical role in maintaining the health of mountain ecosystems. Although the Himalayan griffon has not experienced the same dramatic population declines as other species, it still faces threats from habitat loss and human encroachment.

Conservation programs in countries like India, Nepal, and Pakistan are working to restore vulture populations through captive breeding programs and the establishment of vulture-safe zones, where the use of harmful drugs like diclofenac is strictly banned.

North America

North America is home to two species of vultures: the turkey vulture and the black vulture. Both species are widespread and play an important role in cleaning up the environment. The turkey vulture, in particular, is one of the most common and recognizable vultures in the region, known for its distinctive red head and soaring flight patterns.

Turkey vultures are highly adaptable and can be found from southern Canada to the tip of South America. They are known for their keen sense of smell, which helps them locate carrion, even when it is hidden beneath dense foliage. The black vulture, while more limited in range, is also an important scavenger in the southeastern United States and parts of Mexico.

Both species benefit from human activity in some ways, often scavenging along highways and in agricultural areas. Their populations are stable, and they are not currently considered at risk.

South America

South America is home to several unique vulture species, including the majestic Andean condor, one of the largest flying birds in the world. Found primarily in the Andes Mountains, the Andean condor is a powerful symbol in many South American cultures and plays a critical role in maintaining the balance of high-altitude ecosystems.

In addition to the Andean condor, South America is home to the king vulture, a striking bird with a colorful head that inhabits tropical forests from Mexico to Argentina. King vultures are less common than turkey vultures but play an essential role in scavenging, especially in dense forests where they use their strong beaks to access tough carcasses.

Australia and Antarctica

Interestingly, vultures are entirely absent from Australia and Antarctica. The isolated evolution of Australia's fauna means that the continent developed its own set of scavengers, including wedge-tailed eagles and large crows, which fulfill the ecological role of cleaning up carrion.

Similarly, Antarctica's harsh, icy environment is unsuitable for vultures, as there is little food for scavengers in such a cold and barren landscape.

9. The Role of Vultures in the Ecosystem

Vultures, though often misunderstood or seen as ominous creatures, are indispensable to the ecosystems they inhabit. As nature's cleanup crew, they prevent the spread of diseases, recycle nutrients, and maintain the delicate balance that allows life to thrive. Their ability to consume carrion swiftly and safely makes them one of the most important scavengers in the world, protecting both the environment and the health of other species—including humans.

By playing such a vital role in their ecosystems, vultures ensure that life and death are part of a continuous cycle that sustains all living things. In regions where vultures have declined, the consequences have been profound, underscoring the need for conservation efforts to protect these essential birds. Whether soaring high above the plains or perched on a rocky cliff, vultures are a reminder that every part of nature has its place, and even in death, there is life.

Vultures as Nature's Cleanup Crew

Vultures play a vital role in the ecosystems where they live, often referred to as nature's cleanup crew. These birds are scavengers, meaning their diet primarily consists of dead animals, also known as carrion. While other animals may shy away from decaying flesh, vultures have evolved to thrive on it. Their strong stomach acids allow them to digest carrion that would be harmful to most other creatures, making them incredibly efficient at cleaning up the environment.

The presence of vultures ensures that carcasses do not rot for extended periods, which would otherwise attract a host of insects, bacteria, and other scavengers that may not be as effective at clearing away the remains. Vultures act quickly when they find a carcass, often consuming the bulk of it within hours, which significantly reduces the impact of decomposition on the surrounding environment.

These birds are often seen soaring high in the sky, scanning vast areas with their keen eyesight. When a vulture spots a dead animal, it will descend and begin the process of feeding, sometimes joined by other vultures. This communal feeding not only benefits the vultures but also helps maintain the health of the ecosystem by ensuring that no organic matter is wasted or left to decay.

By consuming the remains of dead animals, vultures contribute to the natural recycling of nutrients, breaking down and returning organic material to the soil, which supports plant growth. In this way, they help sustain the balance of life in their environments, from savannas to forests, deserts to mountains.

How Vultures Help Prevent the Spread of Disease

One of the most critical roles vultures play in the ecosystem is their ability to prevent the spread of disease. Dead animals can be breeding grounds for harmful pathogens such as anthrax, rabies, and botulism, which pose a threat to both wildlife and humans. When vultures consume carcasses, they effectively eliminate these dangerous pathogens from the environment.

The vulture's digestive system is highly specialized for this task. Their stomachs contain strong acids and enzymes that can neutralize bacteria and viruses that would otherwise spread to other animals or enter the water supply. By removing diseased carcasses from the landscape, vultures act as a natural barrier against the transmission of diseases that could lead to epidemics in wildlife populations and even impact human communities living nearby.

In many regions where vulture populations have declined, there has been a noticeable rise in diseases associated with decaying animal remains. Without vultures to efficiently dispose of carcasses, other scavengers, such as feral dogs and rats, move in to take their place. However, these animals are not as well-equipped to handle the pathogens present in rotting meat and can become vectors for disease themselves, spreading illnesses through bites, droppings, or contact with humans.

This decline in vulture populations has had particularly severe consequences in places like South Asia, where the near extinction of vultures due to poisoning has led to an increase in feral dog populations and a subsequent rise in rabies cases. In India, for example, the loss of vultures has been linked to a sharp increase in rabies-related deaths among humans, highlighting just how essential these birds are to maintaining public health.

The Ecological Benefits of Scavenging

Scavenging is an often overlooked aspect of the food chain, but it plays a crucial role in maintaining ecological balance. Vultures are among the most efficient scavengers in the animal kingdom, and their role extends beyond simply removing dead animals. By feeding on carcasses, vultures help regulate predator populations, prevent the spread of diseases, and recycle nutrients back into the ecosystem.

In ecosystems where large predators like lions, wolves, or hyenas are present, vultures help manage the competition for food. When a predator makes a kill, vultures often arrive shortly after to consume the remains, ensuring that nothing goes to waste. This process helps keep predator populations in check, as it limits the amount of food available to them. Vultures, by swiftly consuming carrion, reduce the chance of other dangerous carnivores gathering around the carcass, which can help avoid conflict between predators.

Additionally, vultures contribute to the overall cleanliness of the environment. By disposing of dead animals before they begin to decompose, vultures prevent the buildup of harmful bacteria and toxins in the soil and water. This benefits not only the plants and animals in the immediate area but also the larger ecosystem by maintaining the health of the land and reducing the likelihood of contamination.

Moreover, the nutrients that vultures process from carcasses are returned to the environment in a more manageable form. The remains that vultures leave behind, such as bones, are further broken down by other scavengers or decomposers like insects and fungi, completing the nutrient cycle. This process enriches the soil, promoting plant growth and supporting the overall productivity of the ecosystem.

In some ecosystems, vultures are considered keystone species, meaning their presence and actions have a disproportionately large impact on the health and stability of the environment. Without vultures, many ecosystems would struggle to maintain the balance between life and death, cleanliness and decay.

10. Vulture Conservation: Challenges and Efforts

Vulture conservation is a global effort that requires collaboration between governments, conservationists, and local communities. While vultures face numerous threats, from poisoning to habitat loss, ongoing conservation programs are making a difference. By raising awareness about the importance of vultures, creating safe spaces for them to feed and nest, and addressing the root causes of their decline, these efforts are helping to protect one of nature's most important scavengers.

The story of vulture conservation is not just about saving a single species; it is about protecting ecosystems, preventing disease outbreaks, and maintaining the balance of nature. Vultures may not always be the most celebrated or glamorous animals, but their role in the environment is invaluable, and their survival is linked to the health of the world we all share. Through continued conservation efforts, we can ensure that these vital birds continue to soar in the skies for generations to come.

Why Vulture Conservation is Important

Vultures, often misunderstood or overlooked, are critical to the health of ecosystems around the world. Their role as nature's cleanup crew makes them indispensable in controlling disease and maintaining the balance between life and decay. However, in many regions, vultures are facing severe population declines, putting ecosystems and even human communities at risk. This makes vulture conservation more important than ever.

When vultures disappear, the consequences are far-reaching. Without these scavengers, carcasses are left to decay slowly, leading to the spread of deadly diseases such as anthrax, rabies, and botulism. The absence of vultures can also lead to an increase in populations of feral dogs and rats, which fill the scavenging gap but are less effective at preventing disease transmission. This, in turn, poses a serious threat to human health, especially in regions where livestock plays a central role in the economy and everyday life.

Vultures are also part of intricate food chains. By consuming the remains of dead animals, they help ensure that nutrients are recycled back into the ecosystem, supporting plant growth and sustaining other wildlife. Their presence prevents the build-up of waste and helps control the populations of other scavengers that might otherwise become overabundant. In this way, vultures contribute to the overall health and stability of the environments in which they live.

Beyond their ecological importance, vultures hold cultural significance in many parts of the world. In some regions, they are revered for their role in maintaining cleanliness and order in nature, while in others, they are an integral part of traditional practices, such as sky burials in Tibet. Preserving vultures is not only about maintaining biodiversity but also about protecting cultural heritage and ensuring a healthy future for both humans and wildlife.

Causes of Vulture Decline: Poaching, Poisoning, and Habitat Loss

Unfortunately, vultures are now one of the most threatened groups of birds in the world. Several factors contribute to their decline, including poaching, poisoning, and habitat loss. These threats have driven many vulture species to the brink of extinction, with some now classified as critically endangered.

One of the most significant causes of vulture decline is poisoning. In many parts of Africa and Asia, vultures are accidentally poisoned by chemicals intended for other animals. Farmers, for instance, often use poison to kill livestock predators like lions or hyenas, but when vultures feed on the poisoned carcasses, they become unintended victims. In some cases, entire vulture colonies have been wiped out by a single poisoned carcass.

Another widespread issue is the use of veterinary drugs like diclofenac. This anti-inflammatory drug, commonly used to treat cattle in South Asia, has had a devastating impact on vulture populations. When vultures consume the carcasses of livestock treated with diclofenac, they suffer fatal kidney failure. In countries like India, Nepal, and Pakistan, the use of diclofenac has led to the collapse of vulture populations, with declines of over 90% in some areas.

Poaching is also a problem for vultures, particularly in parts of Africa. In some regions, vultures are killed deliberately by poachers who do not want the birds circling over animal carcasses, which can alert authorities to their illegal activities. In other areas, vultures are hunted for use in traditional medicine, as some cultures believe that consuming vulture parts can bestow special powers or good luck.

In addition to poisoning and poaching, habitat loss poses a significant threat to vultures. As human populations expand, the natural habitats where vultures nest and feed are being destroyed. Urbanization, deforestation, and agricultural expansion are reducing the availability of safe nesting sites and reliable food sources, pushing vultures into areas where they are more vulnerable to human threats.

Conservation Programs and Success Stories

Despite these challenges, there is hope for the future of vultures. Conservation programs around the world are working to protect these birds and reverse their population declines. These efforts range from breeding programs to the creation of "vulture restaurants"—designated feeding stations where vultures can safely find food.

One of the most successful vulture conservation initiatives is the ban on diclofenac in several countries, including India, Nepal, and Pakistan. This ban has been critical in slowing the decline of vulture populations in South Asia, where diclofenac poisoning has wiped out millions of birds. In its place, a safer alternative drug, meloxicam, is now being promoted for use in livestock, helping to protect vultures from accidental poisoning.

Breeding programs have also played a key role in vulture conservation. In regions where vulture populations have become critically low, conservationists have established captive breeding centers. These centers raise vultures in controlled environments, allowing them to breed and reproduce without the risks they would face in the wild. Once the young vultures are strong enough, they are released into protected areas, where they can join wild populations and contribute to the recovery of their species.

Vulture restaurants are another innovative conservation tool. These feeding stations provide safe, poison-free food for vultures in areas where food sources have become scarce or dangerous. By offering a reliable supply of uncontaminated carcasses, vulture restaurants help ensure that vultures can feed without the risk of poisoning. They also help support ecotourism, as tourists can visit these feeding sites to observe vultures in their natural habitats, raising awareness about the importance of vulture conservation.

In Africa, the establishment of vulture-safe zones has proven effective in protecting these birds from poisoning. These zones are areas where the use of poisons and harmful chemicals is strictly regulated, and efforts are made to reduce human-vulture conflicts. These zones also help raise awareness among local communities about the importance of vultures, encouraging people to coexist with these birds rather than seeing them as pests.

One of the most inspiring vulture conservation success stories comes from Spain, where the population of griffon vultures has increased significantly in recent decades. Thanks to strict legal protections, habitat restoration, and the establishment of vulture restaurants, Spain is now home to one of the largest vulture populations in Europe. The country has become a model for vulture conservation, showing that with concerted efforts, these birds can recover and thrive.

11. Vultures in Specific Countries

Vultures face vastly different challenges and successes in different parts of the world. In India, their populations are slowly recovering after a devastating decline caused by poisoning. Europe has seen significant success in vulture conservation, with thriving populations thanks to strong legal protections and public engagement. Meanwhile, Africa's vultures are in crisis, but ongoing conservation efforts hold the potential for a brighter future.

The fate of vultures across the globe is intertwined with human action, and their survival depends on our ability to address the threats they face. Whether through banning harmful substances, creating safe spaces for feeding and nesting, or educating communities about the importance of vultures, there is hope that these essential birds can continue to play their vital role in the ecosystems of the world.

The Status of Vultures in India

India was once home to some of the largest vulture populations in the world, with species like the white-rumped vulture, Indian vulture, and slender-billed vulture being common sights in both urban and rural landscapes. However, over the past few decades, vulture numbers in India have plummeted at an alarming rate. The primary cause of this decline was the widespread use of the veterinary drug diclofenac, which proved to be toxic to vultures that fed on the carcasses of treated livestock.

The impact of diclofenac was devastating. Vultures that consumed even small amounts of the drug through dead cattle suffered from fatal kidney failure, leading to a catastrophic decline in the population. By the early 2000s, India had lost more than 95% of its vulture population, which had far-reaching consequences for both the environment and public health. With fewer vultures to clean up dead animals, the country saw a rise in the number of feral dogs and rats, leading to an increase in diseases like rabies.

In response to this crisis, India took significant steps to address the issue. In 2006, the government banned the use of diclofenac for veterinary purposes and promoted the use of meloxicam, a safer alternative. This ban was a crucial turning point in vulture conservation efforts, and since then, vulture populations in India have shown slow but encouraging signs of recovery.

India has also established breeding centers where vultures are raised in captivity and later released into safe zones. These safe zones are areas where the use of harmful veterinary drugs is strictly regulated, and where vulture populations can gradually rebuild. Conservation organizations, along with government agencies, have also launched public awareness campaigns to educate people about the importance of vultures and the role they play in maintaining a healthy environment.

While vultures in India are not out of danger yet, these conservation efforts have provided hope for the future. The recovery will take time, but the commitment to saving these birds is strong, and the progress made so far is a testament to the power of dedicated conservation action.

Conservation Success in Europe

In contrast to the sharp declines seen in India, Europe has become a beacon of hope for vulture conservation. Over the past few decades, several European countries have successfully implemented conservation programs that have led to a significant rebound in vulture populations, particularly in Spain, France, and Greece.

One of the key success stories in Europe is the recovery of the griffon vulture. Once on the brink of extinction due to habitat loss and poisoning, the griffon vulture population has steadily increased, thanks to a combination of legal protections, habitat restoration, and the establishment of vulture restaurants. These restaurants are designated feeding stations where safe carcasses are provided to vultures, ensuring that they have a reliable food source free from poison.

Spain, in particular, has emerged as a leader in vulture conservation, with one of the largest populations of griffon vultures in the world. The country has created protected areas where vultures can nest and feed without interference from human activity. In addition, Spain has worked to restore natural habitats that had been degraded by agriculture and urban development, providing more suitable environments for vultures to thrive.

The bearded vulture, another species that had faced severe declines in Europe, has also benefited from conservation efforts. Found primarily in mountainous regions like the Pyrenees and the Alps, the bearded vulture population has been bolstered by reintroduction programs that have successfully released captive-bred individuals back into the wild.

Europe's success in vulture conservation is largely due to a combination of strong legal frameworks, public engagement, and collaboration between governments and conservation organizations. By prioritizing the protection of these birds and addressing the threats they face, European countries have created a model for vulture conservation that could be replicated in other parts of the world.

Declining Populations in Africa

Africa, home to some of the world's most iconic vulture species, is facing a vulture crisis. Species like the white-backed vulture, lappet-faced vulture, and hooded vulture, which once soared in large numbers across the continent's savannas and woodlands, are now rapidly disappearing. The reasons for this decline are multifaceted, but the primary drivers include poisoning, habitat loss, and poaching.

Poisoning is perhaps the most serious threat to vultures in Africa. In many parts of the continent, vultures are inadvertently poisoned when they feed on carcasses that have been laced with chemicals intended to kill predators like lions or hyenas. In some cases, poachers deliberately poison carcasses to eliminate vultures, as the birds' habit of circling over dead animals can alert authorities to illegal hunting activities. These incidents can wipe out entire colonies of vultures, with devastating consequences for the ecosystem.

Habitat loss is another significant issue. As human populations in Africa continue to grow, more land is being converted for agriculture and development, reducing the amount of suitable habitat for vultures to nest and feed. Additionally, the decline in large herbivore populations due to poaching and habitat destruction means there are fewer carcasses available for vultures to scavenge.

Poaching for traditional medicine is also contributing to the decline of vultures in some parts of Africa. In certain cultures, vulture parts are believed to have magical properties or medicinal benefits, leading to the illegal capture and killing of these birds. This trade, though small in scale, has a disproportionate impact on already dwindling populations.

Despite these challenges, there are efforts underway to save Africa's vultures. Conservation organizations are working with local communities to raise awareness about the importance of vultures and to reduce human-wildlife conflict. Anti-poisoning campaigns are being launched to educate farmers about the dangers of using poison to kill predators and vulture-safe zones are being established in key areas to provide a haven for these birds.

While the situation remains dire, these efforts offer a glimmer of hope. The key to success in Africa will be collaboration between governments, conservationists, and local communities, ensuring that vultures have the protection they need to survive.

12. Interesting Facts about Vultures

Vultures are truly remarkable creatures, with adaptations and abilities that make them some of the most efficient scavengers in nature. From their specialized beaks and digestive systems to their extraordinary senses of sight and smell, vultures are perfectly designed for their role in maintaining the health of ecosystems. Beyond their physical attributes, vultures have also left an indelible mark on human culture, symbolizing everything from death and decay to protection and renewal.

Their role as nature's cleanup crew ensures that ecosystems remain balanced and free from disease, making them one of the most important birds in the natural world. Whether soaring high in the sky, scanning the ground for food, or featuring in the myths of ancient civilizations, vultures are creatures worthy of fascination and respect.

Unique Adaptations for Scavenging

Vultures are masters of scavenging, with specialized adaptations that allow them to thrive in environments where other animals might struggle. One of their most distinctive features is their bald head, which, while it might appear unusual, serves a very practical purpose. Vultures often feed on the decaying flesh of large carcasses, and their bare heads help them avoid bacteria and blood from sticking to their feathers. This adaptation keeps them cleaner and reduces the risk of infection after feeding.

Their beaks are another key feature in their scavenging success. Unlike the sharp, curved beaks of birds of prey designed for hunting, vultures have strong, hook-like beaks perfect for tearing through tough hide and muscle. This allows them to access the nutritious parts of a carcass that other animals might struggle to reach. Some species, like the lappet-faced vulture, are known to open up carcasses, making it easier for smaller scavengers to feed on the remains.

Vultures' digestive systems are also uniquely adapted to handle their diet. Their stomach acids are extremely strong, capable of breaking down decaying flesh and even bones without causing the bird any harm. This powerful digestive system also allows them to neutralize dangerous pathogens that would be deadly to other animals, making vultures nature's frontline defense against disease.

In addition to these physical adaptations, vultures are highly social scavengers. They often rely on each other to locate food, gathering in large groups around a carcass. This communal feeding behavior ensures that they can quickly and efficiently consume the remains of dead animals, helping to clean up the environment and maintain the balance of nature.

Vultures' Remarkable Sense of Smell and Sight

One of the most fascinating aspects of vultures is their extraordinary ability to find food from great distances, thanks to their incredible sense of sight and, in some species, an exceptional sense of smell.

Old World vultures, which are found in Africa, Europe, and Asia, rely primarily on their sharp eyesight to spot carcasses. These vultures can soar at great heights, scanning vast areas below for any sign of a meal. Their eyesight is so powerful that they can detect the movement of other scavengers, such as hyenas or other vultures, from miles away. Once a vulture spots a potential meal, it will glide down, often attracting other vultures in the process. This keen vision allows them to cover enormous distances in search of food, making them one of the most efficient scavengers in the animal kingdom.

New World vultures, such as the turkey vulture, have an additional advantage: a highly developed sense of smell. Unlike most birds, which have a relatively weak sense of smell, turkey vultures can detect the scent of decaying flesh from miles away, even when the carcass is hidden beneath dense forest cover. This remarkable olfactory ability is made possible by the large olfactory bulbs in the brain, which help them detect ethyl mercaptan, a gas produced by decaying animals.

The combination of keen sight and, in some species, an exceptional sense of smell, ensures that vultures can find food even in environments where other scavengers might struggle. Their ability to locate carcasses quickly helps prevent the spread of disease by removing decaying remains from the ecosystem.

Cultural Myths and Legends Surrounding Vultures

Vultures have been both revered and feared in various cultures throughout history. While they are often associated with death due to their scavenging habits, many civilizations have also viewed vultures as symbols of protection, renewal, and the cycle of life.

In ancient Egypt, vultures were considered sacred and were often associated with the goddess Nekhbet, who was depicted as a vulture. Nekhbet was the protector of Upper Egypt, and she symbolized motherhood, protection, and nurturing. The vulture's wide wings, which seemed to embrace the land, were seen as a symbol of the goddess's care and guardianship over the people and the land.

In Tibetan culture, vultures play a central role in sky burials, a traditional funerary practice where the bodies of the deceased are offered to vultures. This ritual is based on the belief that vultures help the soul of the deceased ascend to the heavens, completing the cycle of life and death. The vultures, in this context, are seen as spiritual intermediaries, helping to release the soul from the body and return it to nature.

However, not all cultures view vultures in a positive light. In some Western folklore, vultures are often seen as harbingers of death or misfortune, likely because they are frequently found near carcasses. Their appearance circling in the sky is sometimes viewed as an ominous sign, signaling that death or disaster is nearby. This negative image has been reinforced by popular media, where vultures are often portrayed as grim or foreboding creatures.

Despite these varying interpretations, vultures have remained a significant symbol in human culture. Whether seen as protectors, guides to the afterlife, or reminders of the inevitability of death, vultures hold a unique place in the myths and legends of many civilizations.

13. Vultures in History and Mythology

Vultures, far from being mere scavengers, have carried deep symbolic meaning across different cultures and time periods. In ancient Egypt, they were protectors and nurturers; in Tibet, they guided souls to the afterlife; in Greece and Rome, they symbolized war, death, and endurance. Through art, literature, and religion, vultures have been woven into the fabric of human understanding of life and death, embodying themes of renewal, transition, and survival.

Their presence in myths and legends reminds us of the delicate balance between life and decay, and their role in religious practices reflects the spiritual importance attributed to them in many cultures. Whether they are depicted as guides to the afterlife, symbols of protection, or reminders of the inevitability of death, vultures remain powerful figures in human history, revered and feared in equal measure.

As we look at vultures in art and literature, we see not just a bird, but a creature that has inspired awe, respect, and contemplation across centuries. Their story is one of survival, both in the natural world and in the human imagination, where they continue to soar as symbols of both life's fragility and its enduring strength.

Symbolism of Vultures in Ancient Cultures

Vultures have held symbolic meaning in human cultures for thousands of years, often embodying themes of life, death, protection, and renewal. In various ancient civilizations, these scavengers were revered not only for their ecological role but also for the deeper spiritual and mythological connotations they carried.

One of the earliest and most significant associations with vultures comes from ancient Egypt, where these birds were closely linked to royalty and divinity. The Egyptian goddess Nekhbet, the protector of Upper Egypt, was often depicted as a vulture. Nekhbet was seen as a symbol of motherhood, nurturing, and protection, particularly for the pharaoh and the people of Egypt. Vultures, with their wide wings and watchful presence, were believed to embody the goddess's protective power, watching over the land and its people. The royal headdress of the pharaoh often included the image of a vulture alongside a cobra, representing both the nurturing and defensive forces in Egyptian society.

In other parts of the ancient world, vultures played different roles. In Tibet, for example, vultures are a vital part of a sacred funerary practice known as sky burial. In this tradition, the bodies of the deceased are offered to vultures, which are seen as spiritual intermediaries. The vultures are believed to help the soul of the deceased ascend to the heavens, completing the cycle of life and death. This practice reflects a deep respect for vultures, acknowledging their role in nature as essential to both the physical and spiritual realms.

In ancient Greece, vultures were associated with the gods of war, particularly Ares. Their appearance on battlefields, feasting on the dead, gave them a grim but respected role in the aftermath of conflict. Similarly, in Roman mythology, vultures were sometimes viewed as harbingers of death and destruction, but they were also seen as symbols of strength and endurance, able to survive in harsh conditions.

Vultures also feature prominently in African folklore, where they are often regarded as wise creatures. In some cultures, vultures are seen as mediators between the living and the dead, offering guidance and insight. Their ability to find sustenance in even the most desolate environments has led to their being admired for their resilience and resourcefulness.

Vultures in Art, Literature, and Religion

Vultures have made their mark not only in mythology but also in art, literature, and religion throughout history. Artists and writers have been drawn to the powerful imagery that vultures evoke—the cycle of life and death, the delicate balance between decay and renewal, and the thin line between the physical and spiritual worlds.

In ancient Egyptian art, vultures were often depicted in royal and religious contexts, reinforcing their association with protection and divinity. Wall carvings, tomb paintings, and sculptures frequently featured vultures alongside other sacred animals, illustrating their revered status. The vulture's image was considered so important that it was included in the crowns of queens and goddesses, a testament to their symbolic power.

Vultures also found a place in classical literature. In Greek tragedies and epics, they were often used as symbols of death and decay. For instance, in Homer's "Iliad," vultures circling above the battlefield were a grim reminder of the inevitable death that awaited the warriors. In Roman literature, poets like Virgil and Ovid used vultures as metaphors for death and fate, emphasizing their connection to the cycle of life and destruction.

In Christianity, vultures are mentioned in the Bible, often in reference to judgment and desolation. In the Book of Revelation, for instance, vultures are described as part of the apocalyptic vision, gathering to feast on the fallen during the final days. While the imagery here is dark, it reflects the deep cultural association between vultures and death, as well as the natural process of decay and renewal.

Religious art from different parts of the world also incorporates vultures. In Tibetan Buddhist art, for instance, depictions of sky burials sometimes feature vultures, emphasizing their role in helping the soul transition from the physical to the spiritual realm. These images are both reverent and pragmatic, illustrating the importance of vultures in religious rites and beliefs.

In more modern art and literature, vultures continue to be used as powerful symbols. They have appeared in works ranging from classic novels to contemporary paintings, often representing both life and death, hope and despair. In Ernest Hemingway's "The Snows of Kilimanjaro," vultures circle ominously around the protagonist, symbolizing his impending death. In contrast, in modern environmental art, vultures are often depicted as symbols of resilience, reflecting their crucial role in maintaining ecological balance.

In many indigenous African and South American cultures, vultures have been featured in tribal art and spiritual practices. For instance, feathers from vultures have been used in rituals and ceremonies, believed to carry special powers due to the bird's connection to both life and death. This belief underscores the vulture's status as a creature that bridges worlds, embodying both destruction and regeneration.

14. Stories and Anecdotes about Vultures

From rural communities relying on vultures to dispose of livestock to scientists tracking their movements in the wild, stories of human-vulture interactions have revealed both the challenges and the fascinating behaviors of these birds. Through research and conservation efforts, we are learning more about vultures' critical role in ecosystems and the importance of protecting them.

The anecdotes from village life, historical tales of superstition, and modern scientific studies all contribute to the rich narrative of vultures as both creatures of mystery and scientific inquiry. The stories about vultures are as diverse as the birds themselves, but they all share one thing in common: a recognition of the essential role these scavengers play in maintaining the delicate balance of nature. As humans continue to interact with vultures—whether through conservation efforts or through shared environments—it is clear that these birds have much to teach us about resilience, survival, and the interconnectedness of all life.

Notable Stories of Human-Vulture Interaction

Vultures have long fascinated humans, not just for their role in the natural world but for the unexpected interactions they've had with people over time. Some of these encounters highlight the birds' intelligence, while others show the complex relationship between humans and these scavengers.

One well-known story comes from South Asia, where vultures were a regular part of village life. In rural India and Nepal, farmers would often leave dead livestock in open fields, knowing that vultures would soon arrive to clean up the remains. This informal system created a symbiotic relationship, where vultures provided a valuable service by keeping the environment clean, and humans ensured a steady supply of food for the birds. In the past, these scenes were so common that locals would refer to vultures as "the village sweepers," playing a vital role in public health by preventing the spread of diseases from decomposing carcasses.

In more recent years, however, human-vulture interactions have become rarer due to the massive decline in vulture populations caused by the use of the veterinary drug diclofenac. The drug, toxic to vultures, led to the near-extinction of several species, changing the dynamic in many rural areas. While the sight of vultures circling over the fields may now be less common, these birds remain a part of the cultural memory of many communities that once depended on their presence.

In Africa, vultures have been both revered and feared. For example, there are stories from Tanzania about how local communities used to view vultures as bad omens, particularly if they were seen circling over villages. People believed that vultures brought bad luck or foreshadowed sickness and death. However, over time, as conservation efforts have grown, many African communities have come to understand the ecological importance of vultures and have begun to protect them.

A more modern and scientific story of human-vulture interaction occurred during the efforts to save the California condor, one of the largest vulture species in the world. By the 1980s, the California condor population had dwindled to just 27 birds due to habitat loss and poisoning. In a bold conservation effort, wildlife experts captured the remaining condors and started a breeding program in captivity. Over several decades, the condor population was carefully managed, and young birds were gradually reintroduced into the wild. Today, thanks to these efforts, there are over 400 California condors, with many living freely in the wild once again.

These stories, whether set in rural villages or modern conservation labs, reveal how closely intertwined vultures and humans have been throughout history. Vultures have influenced human culture, health, and survival, even as humans have played a central role in shaping the fate of these birds.

Research Stories: Studying Vultures in the Wild

Researching vultures in the wild is no easy task. These birds often inhabit remote and rugged terrains, and their scavenging habits make them unpredictable. Yet, studying vultures is crucial for understanding their behavior, their role in ecosystems, and the conservation measures needed to protect them.

One remarkable story comes from the research conducted in Africa's Serengeti National Park, where scientists have spent decades observing the feeding behaviors of vultures. Researchers set up observation stations near known vulture feeding areas and used radio transmitters to track the birds' movements. One of the surprising discoveries from this research was how vultures work together when scavenging. Different species have evolved to fill specific roles within the scavenging process: for example, the powerful lappet-faced vulture is often the first to tear open a carcass, while the smaller white-backed vultures follow to feed on the softer tissues. This cooperation among species ensures that no part of the carcass goes to waste.

Another interesting research story comes from South America, where biologists have studied the Andean condor. The Andean condor, one of the largest flying birds in the world, has long captured the attention of scientists due to its impressive ability to soar for hours without flapping its wings. Researchers have used GPS trackers to follow the movements of these birds, revealing that they can travel hundreds of kilometers in search of food. One condor was recorded flying over 200 kilometers in a single day without flapping its wings more than a few times, relying on thermal updrafts to stay aloft. This research has provided valuable insights into how condors conserve energy, an essential adaptation in the mountainous regions where they live.

Vulture research also extends to understanding how these birds help control disease. In South Asia, a team of scientists has studied how the loss of vultures has affected the spread of rabies. As vulture populations declined due to diclofenac poisoning, feral dog populations surged, leading to an increase in rabies cases. The researchers found that without vultures to quickly dispose of carcasses, the ecosystem's balance was disrupted, creating a public health crisis. This study highlighted the critical role vultures play in preventing the spread of diseases, not just in animals but also in humans.

In the United States, researchers studying the turkey vulture have made some surprising discoveries about their sense of smell. Unlike most birds, which rely primarily on sight, turkey vultures have an acute sense of smell that allows them to detect the scent of decaying flesh from miles away. Using experiments with artificial scents, researchers confirmed that turkey vultures could locate hidden food even in dense forests, a skill that sets them apart from other scavengers. This discovery has opened up new avenues for studying avian olfaction and has deepened our understanding of how vultures navigate their environments.

These stories from the field show that researching vultures is not only about studying the birds themselves but also about understanding the ecosystems they help maintain. By tracking their movements, observing their feeding habits, and studying their role in disease control, researchers are uncovering the vital importance of vultures to the natural world.

15. Conclusion: The Future of Vultures

The journey of vultures from the brink of extinction to a hopeful future mirrors the resilience of nature itself. With ongoing conservation efforts, community support, and global awareness, we can pave the way for a world where vultures continue to play their essential role in maintaining the balance of the natural world. The road ahead is challenging, but the story of vultures is far from over—and their future is in our hands.

The Road Ahead for Vulture Conservation

The future of vultures depends largely on the actions we take today. Vultures, despite their essential role in ecosystems, are among the most threatened bird species in the world. With many vulture populations declining rapidly due to habitat loss, poisoning, and human activity, the road ahead for their conservation is steep but not impossible.

One of the most crucial steps for vulture conservation is the continued effort to ban harmful substances, like diclofenac, which have caused devastating declines in vulture populations, particularly in South Asia. In regions where these bans are already in place, there is promising evidence that vulture populations are beginning to stabilize. However, the enforcement of these bans and the promotion of safe alternatives, such as meloxicam, remain key to ensuring that vultures do not face further risks from veterinary drugs.

Conservation programs around the world are already making a difference. In Europe, for instance, the success of vulture breeding programs and the establishment of protected areas have led to a resurgence in species like the griffon vulture and the bearded vulture. Similar efforts are taking root in other regions, where vulture-safe zones are being created to protect both the birds and their habitats.

Education and public awareness campaigns also play a vital role in vulture conservation. By informing people about the importance of vultures and dispelling myths that portray them negatively, we can foster a culture of coexistence. Communities that once viewed vultures as bad omens or pests are learning to appreciate their critical role in maintaining the health of ecosystems. Encouraging local involvement in conservation efforts, particularly in rural areas where human-wildlife interactions are common, is essential for the long-term protection of vultures.

Another promising approach is the creation of vulture restaurants, where safe carcasses are provided for vultures to feed on without the risk of poisoning. These feeding stations not only support vulture populations but also help monitor the health of the birds, allowing conservationists to detect early signs of trouble. They have proven successful in countries like Spain and India, and their expansion into other regions could help mitigate the risks vultures face.

Despite the challenges, the future of vulture conservation is hopeful, with many success stories already emerging. Continued international cooperation, research, and local conservation efforts will be key to securing a future where vultures can thrive once more.

How Humans Can Coexist with Vultures

Coexisting with vultures is not only possible but also beneficial for both humans and the environment. These birds play a critical role in keeping ecosystems clean by consuming carcasses that would otherwise rot and spread disease. By understanding the importance of vultures, we can create an environment where humans and vultures live in harmony.

One of the most important aspects of coexistence is reducing human-related threats to vultures. This means addressing issues like poisoning, habitat destruction, and illegal hunting. Farmers and herders can be educated about the dangers of using poisons to kill predators, and alternative methods of livestock protection can be promoted. By eliminating the use of poisons that inadvertently harm vultures, we can significantly reduce the number of deaths caused by contaminated carcasses.

At the same time, protecting the habitats where vultures nest and feed is crucial. Vultures prefer remote, undisturbed areas, but as human development expands, these areas are becoming increasingly scarce. By creating protected zones, particularly in regions where vultures are known to breed and roost, we can ensure that these birds have safe spaces to thrive. This also benefits local biodiversity, as vultures help maintain the balance of ecosystems by preventing the buildup of disease-carrying carcasses.

Public education is another key to successful coexistence. In many cultures, vultures have been misunderstood or even feared. By raising awareness about their role in nature and the threats they face, people can begin to see vultures as valuable members of the ecosystem. Schools, local communities, and governments can work together to promote vulture-friendly practices, such as setting up vulture-safe zones or supporting local conservation efforts.

Finally, ecotourism can play a role in fostering coexistence between humans and vultures. In countries where vultures are making a comeback, tourists are increasingly interested in observing these majestic birds in the wild. By promoting vulture-watching tours and supporting conservation-based tourism, local communities can benefit economically while also contributing to the protection of vultures.

Final Thoughts on Vultures' Place in the Natural World

Vultures hold a unique place in the natural world, serving as vital scavengers that help maintain the balance of ecosystems. Their role is often underappreciated, but without them, the consequences for both wildlife and human communities would be dire. By swiftly consuming the remains of dead animals, vultures prevent the spread of disease, control the population of other scavengers, and recycle nutrients back into the environment.

The decline of vulture populations in many parts of the world is a warning sign about the broader health of ecosystems. When vultures disappear, it signals that something is wrong—whether it's the presence of harmful chemicals, habitat destruction, or human interference. Protecting vultures is not just about saving a single species; it's about preserving the intricate web of life that depends on them.

The future of vultures depends on our willingness to act. Conservation efforts have shown that recovery is possible, but it requires a concerted, long-term commitment from governments, scientists, and local communities. By addressing the threats vultures face and fostering a culture of coexistence, we can ensure that these remarkable birds continue to soar through our skies for generations to come.

In the end, vultures are not just symbols of death or decay; they are symbols of life's resilience and the delicate balance that sustains all living things. Their survival is a testament to the power of nature to heal and regenerate when given the chance. As we look to the future, we must remember that protecting vultures is about more than saving birds—it's about safeguarding the health of our planet and all the creatures that depend on it, including us.

***

****